PAINTED DAYDREAMS

Painted Daydreams
Collection of Ekphrastic Poems

by
B. Elizabeth Beck

Accents Publishing • Lexington, Kentucky • 2019

Copyright © 2019 by B. Elizabeth Beck
All rights reserved

Printed in the United States of America

Accents Publishing
Editor: Katerina Stoykova
Cover Photo: Vincent van Gogh, *Almond Blossoms,* 1890

ISBN: 978-1-936628-50-6
First Edition

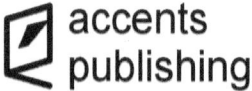

Accents Publishing is an independent press for brilliant voices. For a catalog of current and upcoming titles, please visit us on the Web at

www.accents-publishing.com

CONTENTS

For Vincent / 1

I.

Mirror / 5
Ars Poetica / *Writer's Block (Go Around)* / 6
Kandinsky *Composition IV* / What Is True? / 7
Howls and Hails / 8
A Ready-Made Poem / 9
Not Abstraction / 10
Action Paintings / 11
Iconoclasts / 13
Street Peddler / 14
World's First Rockband / 15
Enigma / 16

II.

Sunflowers / 19
Joyful Exit / 20
Victor Over Medieval Misogyny / 21
The Viriditas of Hildegard of Bingen (1098–1179) / 22
Venus of Willendorf / Charmed Stone / 23
Mother of American Modernism / 24
A Woman's Shepherd / 25
La Vie Bohème as seen in *L'Absinthe* / 26
One of Three / 27
Oxymoronic Feminist / 28

III.

Harmony in Red: A Love Song / 31
Tumbling out / 32
Bedroom in Arles Winter 1888 / Letter to Vincent / 33
My Heart Sings for You, Marc Chagall / 34
Perchance to Dream, Gypsy Poet of the Art World / 35
Follow the Signs / 36
Cave of Lascaux / Life Lessons / 37

Canvas Snoopy Backpack / 38
Darling Hieronymus, / 39
Pyramids of Giza / 40
Egyptology / 41
Ode to a Roman Sarcophagus Showing Dionysus ... / 42

IV.

The Arnolfini Marriage Jan van Eyck 1434 / Strange Reflection / 47
Born on the Same Day / 48
Interruption / 49
Underpainter of the Blue Riders / 50
de Kooning Affair / 51
Rent / 52
Misstep / 53
Happy Birthday, Dorothea / 54
It's Jerry Garcia's Birthday, John / 55
Carnival of Harlequin / Dare Dream / 56
Kindred Spirits / 57

V.

Ancora Imparo / 61
Patch-Eyed Glass Smith / 62
Oh, Munch, What Were You Thinking / 63
Garden of My Hospital / 64
In Ancient Greece, Sophists / 65
Sunday Afternoon at the Museum / 66
Saturday Evening / 67
I Stumble Upon *Les Demoiselles d'Avignon* / 68
For All the World / 69
Twittering Machine / 71
Mad Man / 72
Emperor / 73
What Exactly Is Seurat's Point? / 74
Flux of Living / 75
Abstract Loss / 76

Basquiat! Radiant Child / 77
Fourth Dimension / 78
Good Night / 79
Could This Be True? / 80
Instruct / 82

Resources / 85

Acknowledgments / 91

About the Author / 93

FOR VINCENT

I seek you in every
iris. You taught me
to reach backwards.

I had no idea
it would foreshadow
a lifetime of research.

I.

MIRROR

> Poetry surrounds us everywhere, but putting it on paper is, alas, not so easy as looking at it.
>
> —18 March 1883 letter to Theo

How many self-portraits are enough?
Rembrandt created almost one hundred.
Were you trying to meet his goal?
Or was it that poverty bred necessity?

Perhaps poets should take note to explore
one's self so intently. Purchase a mirror
good enough to study introspection
spending hours learning to hone craft.

I do not want to spend any more hours
writing about my life. I prefer to breathe
art and scribble awe about your
painted daydreams instead.

ARS POETICA
Writer's Block (Go Around)

I will, John Lackey,
I will (go around)
because words pool within
my mind and stones catch
ideas I want to hold between
my teeth. So, instead I gnaw
on the end of my pen not waiting
for the flow. I will accept
a trickle/force scribbles
even when leaves clog autumnal
memories, I will cough/sputter
nonsense (around and around)
on the page until the dam
bursts and ideas flood.

Poets need to walk barefoot
in rivers and suffer/risk
toes whitened/wrinkled if only (just)
to feel/shock the senses because
writing is not (just) a senseless task
even as I wonder what I'm really
doing with my time borrowed
against the ticking of the clock
behind my left shoulder.
I have no choice but to (go around).

Kandinsky *Composition IV*
WHAT IS TRUE?

I taste color, too
understand how sight and sound
confound the senses when I see
music and smell sculptures as you
hear compositions abstracted not
representing anything other than
what pleases you as you fall to
your knees and weep to see
your own painting on its side.

I would have introduced
you to John Lackey but he wasn't
even born before you died and I cringe
remembering when I commented
on background music in Lackey's film
as whiny, not knowing it was his own
and take heart in his gracious assurance
that anonymity breeds honest criticism
I know that to be true, as well.

Phish scorned
as *pissing in audience's ears,* yet I can't applaud
enough when Trey forgets lines much like
Jerry Garcia often stumbled and we loved him
even more for it, that is true. But I wonder
what mantra to chant to write a sonnet
and what wounds behind closed doors
to muffle so that I can even write
one good line before I'm done.

HOWLS AND HAILS

            Ogre   of the art world
     sneered by   the Salon.

Cézanne, you   had courage   to paint

     every day   in obscurity, not
retreating   in shame,   but instead

       seeking   truth in beauty
 nature   rendered   geometric   objects

         deconstructing   form   into its most pure
sense,   misunderstood   until almost

     too late,   yet tenacity displayed

inspires me   to submit   yet another
      poem,
              if only to be declined.

A READY-MADE POEM

> I don't believe in art. I believe in artists.
>
> —Marcel Duchamp

Running on sidewalk, sneakers silently pounding,
I call my dog and can't hear my own voice—
ponder the question redundant
marvelous inexplicable Beethoven
who heard the music as loudly as I blast
Phish in my ears, it occurs to me—

the risk necessary to compose genius:
listen to nothing and assemble everything.
There is no original language—
only divine voices worth studying
searching for recognition making

me laugh at the page exploding Whitman's
barbaric yawp and Ginsberg's *Howl* descending
Saul's galactic journey in the spot
where truth echoes seeking
feminism beyond Jong searing
song lyrics dividing skies melting
the yellow brick road into Pink Floyd's dark
side of the moon. Flaming Lips purse as the flea
flits from John Donne's metaphysical mind
for whom the bell tolls Hemingway haunts
the same streets in Key West I linger kissing

metaphors stumbling over my own Dadaist
tendencies embracing my absurd understanding
of reality blurring my vision—
haphazard compositions plot curves knighted
by Marcel Duchamp secreting doors
while all the while pretending earnest—
defiance makes me love him even more.

NOT ABSTRACTION

Arp, how funny   scattered   litter

     emerges   in your imagination
     as compositions

     you call

     organic concretions
     according to the law of chance.

I am amused

     by accidents.

Happy   your muse lured
     discarded,   torn   pieces

     to assemble   in your

     own accord.

ACTION PAINTINGS

Shattering
a table
full
of glasses,
finger
shards
dip
blood
in designs
after
pounding
surface
so hard,
a box of
matches
bursts
into flame

cannot
attack
keys
of grand
piano
with
ice pick
after
brawling
in bars,
pissing
in potted
plants,
ripping
doors

off
hinges

crashing
car
in fatal
wreck
to destroy
art
because
    energy made visible
can only
exist
in nature
claim
comes
from
within
frenzied
sloshing,
pouring,
dripping
chaos
on canvas
rolled on
barn floors
demanding
new
techniques
seeking
truth
to expand
the universe
in color

ICONOCLASTS

> When my heart beats, it screams thug life.
>
> —Tupac Shakur

Caravaggio and Whitman both rooted in mud
rolled around derelict in bars with Hemingway
fighting and drinking to make art/beauty original
daring to intentionally shock/offend/fuck convention
evil genius/bohemian tendencies leading/beckoning

warrior Artemisia to devote her life painting howling
women who wreak violence against men monsters
who have wronged women in defiance to torture
agony of thumbscrews endured, refusing to recant
lie down/held down by Cosimo in a painful/humiliating trial
against her rapist Tassi naming her art teacher/deflowering
her daring to stain her brilliance/talent telling Judith's story
in gory detail/learned honesty and artistic technique

in Caravaggio's audacity to use a drowned swollen corpse
as model to depict the Madonna revered/beloved virgin
mother's blasphemous bare feet exposed/preferred fetish
audacity over classical ideals of beauty the parish expected
demanded/refused to pay commission, no matter to pay
tavern debts in blow jobs would not be obscene in Key West's
bath houses Hemingway instead penetrated egos not enough
to escape family legacy of suicide/a shot gun propelled
by genetic mutations/inescapable inevitability and alcoholic
rants Caravaggio favored in style/chiaroscuro engaging
il tenebroso/dark manner resulting in death tragically
mundane from fever escaping pardon from the Pope
rescinding unnecessary/unfulfilled death warrant

STREET PEDDLER

> You say it's a living, we've all gotta eat.
>
> —Robert Hunter

he scrawls abstract
portraits of Hemingway
reminiscent of Picasso
as we talk about Bukowski,
I gaze at his sidewalk exhibit,
watercolor landscapes one side,
portraits on the other—

each cubist rendition unique
enough to catch my attention
a moment more, lingering long
enough for him to grace me
with a poem of his own about
a girl from Sweden who left lipstick
smudges behind in Key West
where he drinks vodka in her
memory, writing poetry in her wake

WORLD'S FIRST ROCKBAND

> Whatever you do, take care of your shoes.
>
> —Trey Anastasio

Stonehenge unlike Gamehendge
where Phish leads us in play
yet were those boulders arranged
in maze to confuse ancient souls
to lose their minds without compass
to guide earth's rotation around sun
much like we drive around cornfields
in psychedelic quests for understanding
keys to universe and answers in souls
lost and found between guitar solos
sometimes stuck to bottom of soles
where Ada Limón keeps all her words
avoiding sharks I have found on the lot
one finger lifted in search of miracle
left-over wishes Jerry Garcia's legacy
ironic lost finger in childhood accident
no excuse to not capture the muse soaring
lyrics Phish never quite mastered
although we love them almost as much

ENIGMA

I scour your letters
to Theo, searching
eviscerated skeleton
keys you possess.
I've yearned to open
secret sacred text.

II.

SUNFLOWERS

not cliché

for a seven-year-old

girl instructed to choose

a still-life to emulate

smelling oil
paint & turpentine

feeling joy

covering canvas waiting

patiently for layers to dry

skimming pages searching

for blue eyes & red beard:
a now-familiar face

JOYFUL EXIT

Looking like a sunflower
sitting upright, blaze
of fire ring around your
head because cremation
not enough to damp spark
of life that compelled two
hundred paintings savagely
portraying women's pain
because you knew

suffering surgeries and bed-
ridden (although perhaps
you enjoyed the bed), daring
marriage tumultuous passion
tumbling sheets soiled by mis-
carriages too many for one
woman to endure, embracing
existence la vie bohème necessary
until you (perchance) chose your end

VICTOR OVER MEDIEVAL MISOGYNY

> If you would reflect well and wisely, you would realize that those events you regard as personal misfortunes have served a useful purpose even in this worldly life, and indeed have worked for your betterment.
>
> —Christine de Pisan, (c. 1365–c. 1463)

Venetian-born   daughter

of astrologer   dreams not of stars

abandons ballads to her dead   husband

    sustaining her children through lines of verse
    imagining *The Book of the City of Ladies* heroic
    extolling the virtues of Joan martyred
    pouring her heartbreak of losing a   child

into volumes of text

    championing women by creating

the weird idea they were   human

THE VIRIDITAS OF HILDEGARD OF BINGEN (1098–1179)

~ The Word is living, being, spirit, all verdant greening, all creativity. This Word manifests itself in every creature.

I look to you,   divine   mystic   Benedictine   abbess

for the   truth of your visions proven

wise and recorded in an original

alphabet constructing a new language

     necessary in order to teach

     not only is the universe an egg (within the womb of god)

     deliver the lesson   phish already taught me

music is   the sacred

language   to best connect human

heart beat and breath with   god

when many times throughout the day I

     fall out of sorts

the green   monophonic chants

will lead me back

integrate   mind,   heart,

          body   and   soul   to heal

Venus of Willendorf
CHARMED STONE

They knew   sacred pebble
to be magic   and collected first
smooth stones to hold
         (for pleasure of round)

warmth in center of palms
until one creative being   formed

         Venus whose naval natural

cavity of original stone
center point of composition
charms in easing birth pains

         (or perhaps merely objects of exchange)

mystery   of the goddess
         haunts folk tales, fables
         Sumerian creation myths

world arising from
passion between   this god

of fresh water   and that god
of salt water

forming the sphere
found in folds and curves
of her figure   no   cosmic drama

reverence sprinkled in gold dust
crystal illumination of power
incubate form when divine spirit

breathes   life

MOTHER OF AMERICAN MODERNISM

Deny claims
      feminists attach
           to your velvet
                petals. Insist
                                you merely
                        sought to
                  magnify beauty
New Yorkers
      too busy
            to notice. Escape
                          to desert
                  New Mexico
            dust with young
lover. Travel
      years alone. Break
            down when work stalls.   Live
            longer than eyesight lasts. Rest
                in ashes scattered
                over
                far
                a
                w
                a
                y.

A WOMAN'S SHEPHERD

> To [my father's] doctrines I owe my great and glorious ambition for the sex to which I proudly belong and whose independence I shall defend until my dying day.
>
> —Rosa Bonheur

I had to learn to celebrate the cow
when first, I became a mother and

then, dragged kicking and screaming
to Kentucky where pastoralism no

longer a fleeting afternoon spent
on Shakedown Street at Grateful Dead

shows, but a lifetime of Bluegrass. I
would drive my son home from school

past the farms to look for *our* cows
my son imagined creating sunglasses

big enough to fit their brown cow eyes
and I would laugh when I first taught

your art to teenagers, calling you and me
both *friend of the cow*. I did not know

at the time that you were also a feminist,
smoking cigarettes and cutting your hair

short. And it is not without irony that I,
too, believe all animals to have a soul.

Even as I cut into my steak.

LA VIE BOHÈME AS SEEN IN L'ABSINTHE

> What in the world ever became of sweet Jane? She lost her sparkle, you know she isn't the same.
>
> —Grateful Dead

she gazes at the wormwood liquor
green oblivion available in the café
where bohemians sit for comfort
mutual understanding solitary
hours necessary to sustain passion

discipline wages war in wrinkled eyelids
despair too familiar washed down in one

swallow after he places a sugar cube
on her tongue to dissolve psychedelic
principles, outraging the Salon audience

labeling her whore for being honest
even as she is a thespian, trained in the art
of deception and he is merely a printer
practiced to scrawl script backwards

shadows of the back of their heads
mirrored behind, leaving reflections
of their melancholy souls, the audacity
of subject Degas chose to paint

ONE OF THREE

> No woman has the right to draw like that.
>
> —Edgar Degas

When I study your paintings
of mother and child, sharply

inhaling recognition of intimacy
found between me and my baby, I

thank you for befriending Degas
in Paris and wonder if you were

a mother, too, Mary Cassatt. Fleeing
the Allegheny and protesting

convention, your work misunderstood
as conservative. Yet no Pieta graces

your compositions. Instead, you embraced
feminist ideals years before it was in

fashion. Even when your father and
a fire attempted to destroy your talent,

you fought to honor gifts bestowed
upon you. I'm so grateful you lived

to see the woman's right to vote.

OXYMORONIC FEMINIST

Judy Chicago, did you actually say
someday when we all grow up, there will be no labels?
I wonder if that is true. You chose not to exhibit
at any show labeling artists by identity, yet irony
has a strange sense of humor. *Chicago* the name
you claimed when denouncing patriarchal links
in your grief of losing both your husband and father,
yet the city was seized by men to control trade
(although I like the idea your surname adopted
because of your thick accent) and its ring echoes
through the Brooklyn Museum where *The Dinner Party*
resides. Celebrating feminist and historical women
using thirty-nine place settings and 999 other names
inscribed, strange design of domestic arts as statement
accessible to any housewife embroidering power
in careful placement. Perhaps Mary Wollstonecraft
would appreciate your triangular display when she
insisted upon *A Vindication of the Rights of Women*
and I wonder if her name is found at your table. She
would have appreciated the domain of home belonging
to women. For women. Of women. About women. If
only just to serve dinner for our husbands and sons.

III.

HARMONY IN RED: *A LOVE SONG*

Because you no longer languish
in blue, she contemplates the fruit
head bowed in concentration
decanters of wine await arrival
lemons scatter across the surface
flat pattern of fabric does not fold
nor does the landscape recede
through the open window, yet
the world is not flat, Henri. Your
wild fauvism fantasy of texture
without shape and colors almost
garish in their jarring juxtaposition
no shadows, depth. Where does the line
between tablecloth and wallpaper divide
from each other and why does it matter?
As long as the wallpaper isn't yellow.

TUMBLING OUT

of Maxims
that Saturday
evening
half-drunk
on matrimony

we did not
expect
to ride
the Ferris wheel
seemingly
appointed

by our shared
delight
to view
the Eiffel Tower
from Chagall's
perspective

but it became
the defining
moment
of golden
pleasure
I tuck into
our scrapbook

Bedroom in Arles Winter 1888
LETTER TO VINCENT

> I dream my painting, and then I paint my dream.
>
> —Vincent van Gogh 6 April 1875

Vincent,
you found your place
in this small, sparse room
blue walls, red blanket
a table holds a brush and bowl.
Whose paintings grace your walls?

I want to walk across floorboards
scarred, scratched, dented by so
many other residents to reach you
lying in bed. I long for your red
beard and blue eyes. No need

to listen without one ear. I
will whisper into the other.

MY HEART SINGS FOR YOU, MARC CHAGALL

Two lovers float
beneath musicians
surrounding
love and beauty
found in moonlight.

White marble
suspended
in night sky
as flutist plays,
Dionysus sings
passion reflected
beside Eiffel Tower.

I so want to ride
a Ferris wheel
in Paris once again.

PERCHANCE TO DREAM, GYPSY POET OF THE ART WORLD

> what dreams may come
>
> —William Shakespeare

                              Your stained glass bathed
                                 blue across my belly
                             six months swollen pregnant
                           I turned the corner as the sun
                     slanted just so and was stunned:
                       inhaled sharply in recognition
                         a color I have always known
                         as a contraction new to me
                        foreshadowed the best art I
                          have ever made. My sun.

FOLLOW THE SIGNS

> Art does not reproduce the visible, it makes visible.
>
> —Paul Klee

key of life deceptive
simplistic designs
reduce compositions
consciously directing
form ambiguous only
unless a newborn

primitive paintings
imitating dream-
like magic of school
children's scribbles
not needing verbal
interpretation of line

patchwork planes
bound by ideograms,
forgotten language,
constellation patterns
echo of runes like
tree roots' inspiration

Cave of Lascaux
LIFE LESSONS

Chasing the dog
into the hole
school boys stumble

upon an underground
chamber irresistible
mystery to hunt

perhaps with the American's
Tom Sawyer in mind?
Their bounty carved

permanently in pages
of every history book
clever teachers use as

mnemonic anecdote
which is really more the magic
than the primitive scrawling

of a hunt ritualistic
the neighborhood boys'
discovery evidence

miracle in the middle
of world war, children
still wander and play

CANVAS SNOOPY BACKPACK
for Clevelle

contains jar of turpentine
slowly seeping, I smell

familiar scent with glee
foreshadowing weekly

after-school art lesson
at teacher's house just

uphill, around bend, I
pedal bicycle determined

to escape in still lives.
Charcoal and oil paint

stain fingers I use
to push blonde bangs

to see more clearly
as time dissolves

with paintbrushes swirled
on canvas stretched

over frames defining
my reality.

DARLING HIERONYMUS,

a mystery how little is known of you
name as strange as your irrational imagery
a world of fantastic dreams depicted
in a *Garden of Earthly Delights* Dr. Seuss
and the twentieth century surrealists study

I pine to frolic with muscleless creatures
amid gigantic fruits, fish and clams erotic
despite your lack of explicit pornography
my imagination supplies desire as central
force in human thought divided triptych

> *Left:*
> Garden of Eden God introduces
> Adam to Eve in front of a fountain
> giraffes, elephants, grotesque creatures
> strange rock formations in the distance
>
> *Center:*
> Orgy of desire original sin
> metaphorical birds and fruit explosion
> within bubbles and carnal machinery
> entangled limbs intertwined fascination
>
> *Right:*
> the fall from Grace leaves no possibility
> of Salvation, moralistic sermon one
> interpretation too pedantic explanation
> lacking knowledge of secret heretical sect

you left no letters nor diaries to trace
understanding leaving me pondering your medieval
surrealist paintings intriguing as puzzles
into a genius mind unintentionally celebrating
what you were supposed to be condemning

PYRAMIDS OF GIZA

Even though the hook they used
to remove the brains through
the nose freaks me out, I do
love my grandmother's scarab
bracelet we did not bury with her.

Instead, I lost it. The stone
sarcophagus isolates masked
mummies with gleaming gems
teetering in eye sockets.
Five-toed naked cats spool
figure eights around crumbling
granite intended to withstand heart-
breaks ingrained in hieroglyphics
inventorying life in minute detail

does not stave off the inevitability
of mortality. As the Great
Sphinx roars Nefertiti's brilliance
and Cleopatra's beautiful kohl-
lined violet eyes lead by Isis before
meeting Osiris disguised as ancient
animal spirits, the Kush empire
blazes golden after Alexander
the Great lead Egypt as pied piper
into the Hellenistic world.

EGYPTOLOGY

Shakespeare's fascination less creepy
than Napoleon's rape the year before 1800

38,000 troops & 175 academics
artists, linguists, scholars invade

Rosetta Stone absconded
as trophy of their spoils

ODE TO A ROMAN SARCOPHAGUS SHOWING DIONYSUS, THE SEASONS, AND OTHER FIGURES
c. A.D. 220–230 Marble. Metropolitan Museum of Art

she simply isn't hungry anymore
wants only to drink cool, clear water she trusts
breathe prayers in the wind

he whispers in her ear, *pretend to be eating flowers*
run your tongue across your lips to taste the nectar

she agrees to sample roses: cherries and blackberries,
pears and strawberries, raspberries and quince
discarding the apple on principle

he breathes against her neck, *almonds, pecans and walnuts*
the edible seeds of drupe fruits. chew and swallow the petals of the fruits

he does not confess removal of leathery flesh at harvest

she cannot abide to render flesh

> *flowers and air and nuts and prayer and water*
> *water and prayer and nuts and air and flowers*

and wine because Bacchus cannot be satisfied without

she dreams of him
when fireflies replace flutterbys
her senses hypnotized in the space
between flickering lights

she dreams the truth
awakens to brew pine needle tea
faces shame of her carnivorous passion
fruit is part of a flowering plant
evolved from ovaries of the flower

water and prayer and nuts and air and flowers
flowers and air and nuts and prayer and water

succulent temptations of fleshy fruit-like growths
sublimate her obsession with his seduction

he approaches her covered in ivy and dripping
in honey, nectar collected by bees from flowers

he holds a fennel staff adorned with a pinecone
her tea needles and his pinecone picked from the same tree

he offers, *take my thyrsus, it is not a weapon, but a beneficent wand*

she lifts her flute and breathes until the trees dance in accordance to her tune

IV.

The Arnolfini Marriage Jan van Eyck 1434
STRANGE REFLECTION

He looks with piety
as she looks down

swollen with maternity
requires matrimony

but I wonder where
love is lost within

pale faces holding hands
almost without touching

perhaps the reflection
in mirror reveals truth

yet Van Eyck's own hand
I was here mocks tradition

beneath brass chandelier
a dog grabs the edge

of her gown and growls
animalistic intentions should

be honored, not ignored

BORN ON THE SAME DAY

the first time they kissed
her passion broke his tooth

the first time she laughed
she breathed his Bulgarian passion

he was determined
she sublimated herself

she wanted not his matrimony
how very French—he said

he should not be left alone
wraps his grief the way he

once wrapped her portrait
turned her flaming hair iconic

in surrounding islands with pink
decorating trees and the Berlin Wall

dotting Japan with blue umbrellas
tragic yellow in California

realizing their homeland dream
Central Park's saffron flowing gates

her name never found
irrelevant they always flew

in separate planes.

INTERRUPTION

> Our dialogue, which leads to the definition of a project, may take place anywhere ….
>
> —Claes Oldenberg

after thirty-two years of marriage,
you are left alone with public
sculptures to weep private grief

how far from five sculptures sold
for twenty-five dollars, your millions
no consolation conversation stopped

before you had the last word, she
had the last breath, leaving you
bereft remembering the trowel

you made for her, she did not like
so you changed color from silver
to bright blue in romantic gesture

she followed you to New York,
through the Guggenheim to
Los Angeles where her pink battle

defeated her critic soul and silenced
her voice, leaving echoes behind
forty sculptures she called *diagnoses*

UNDERPAINTER OF THE BLUE RIDERS

> I have now forgotten who was responsible for the original idea.
>
> —Gabriela Münter

He paints over your composition
hidden beneath layers discovered

too many years later by curators
marveling at reasons unexplained

no more hostile than loving you
while still married, then divorcing

only to marry someone else
he had only just met after twelve

years you spent intertwined
hiding art during war

perhaps if you had continued
painting on glass, you would

have been found before

DE KOONING AFFAIR

Cigarette, she demands.
You immediately comply
unwittingly causing
her eventual demise. After

years took their toll,
your dementia progressed
too far to learn
of your wife's death.

RENT

As long as I drown at the same time, I don't care. But we felt distinctly enough that her life and my life are as one.

—letter to Theo

    Canvas soaks color   Theo weeps letters
  the brilliant multitude   that cannot gesso peace
  of your madness, Vincent   confused linseed

    you smeared paint   passion and agony
    barbaric eruptions   she gave her body
    exquisite detail   so you could paint
    fineness of line   neither of you
    confident   affords rent

    blue eyes beneath   desperation prompts
    fiery brows   separation of souls
  peer through blindness   you defy death days

    malady Sien's gift   after destroying
        what was
    left to you   of your mind
    in return   with a revolver

  your earlobe mailed   She waited miserably
    drowned   in the river
    to prove you   only listened
    to her   much as you predicted

    Paul left

MISSTEP

                    Gaugin, before you
                   fled Paris, did you read
                the Lawrence story of the sun
               when you must have dreamed
           of beach warmth on gray afternoons
           while you glanced up from the page
             to look between raindrops? Tahiti
             the idea you confused with Greece
                where Lawrence set his short
                 story. That's a big mistake.

HAPPY BIRTHDAY, DOROTHEA

locked eye beams across
chessboard launches love
lasting surrealistic thirty-
four years begun in dual
ceremony in Hollywood

insomnia and widowhood
turns your attention to
verse meticulously crafted

your life a *landscape
of wild fantasy* between
Europe and your home
you return because *there
is more than meets the eye*
when *We're All in It Together*

IT'S JERRY GARCIA'S BIRTHDAY, JOHN

I walk across guitar neck from one
side of the creek to the other wondering
what music fills the forest you render

in colors Mother Nature could not conspire
yet, you find in your perceptive nature
blues more vivid and reds deeper, making

my heart weep with joy to stop and breathe
air made sweet with paint, music, scarlet
begonias and sugar magnolias dance

to creek's song balancing instrument
rooted deeply within trunks of trees
gnarled by Kentucky-aged winds blow

through the back of my memories into
a painting I have never seen before

Carnival of Harlequin
DARE DREAM

Your stomach full of radishes
sours breath belched in heart-
broken exhaustion in attempt
to conquer the world with cat
at your side. I must inquire,
when did you celebrate?
Did Lent pass by without notice
when you were tortured
by unrequited love? Chasing
dreams too surreal to explain
meaning abstract academic analysis
pale compared to whimsical ladders
who can hear and I wonder how
to escape out the window to reach
a black and white sun and what
would happen if I leaned in to shake
that white-gloved hand where insects
are freed to hover above such strange
creatures between musical notes
that float and stars hover under
a ceiling because all I can see
are walls and floor. Two planes
enough to capture composition of chaos.

KINDRED SPIRITS

> Since I'm feeling myself again, now I really don't consider myself defeated.
>
> —letter to Theo 7 May 1888

Nor do I, Vincent.
Nor do I.

V.

ANCORA IMPARO

Search the natural world for inspiration,
Neo-Platonic master to God. Your life
devoted to the children of your imagination
forsaking matrimony for immortality.

The stonecutter and his wife could never
imagine the impression on your six-year-old
senses overcoming tragedy of losing your mother
would influence all of Western civilization.

Sculptor, architect, poet breathing
damp mold, crumbling plaster four years
on scaffolding to paint, an inferior form of art
you even returned twenty years later to complete.

On your deathbed, almost ninety years of life
regret only for the work you could not fulfill
a statue so different, I must look at it slant
wondering what alphabet you were just learning.

PATCH-EYED GLASS SMITH

Instead of spending your time
in Venice, kissing under every
bridge, you sailed to Murano
to study glass to change course
of your art forever. Even when
eye lost through shattered
windshield and shoulder damaged,
you did not forsake your work.
Perhaps in attempt to replace the brother
you lost in war and your father a year
after from heart attack, you gathered
a team to collaborate, influenced
by Warhol's Factory you admired
to lift Pollock's paintings from canvas
to render them into actions influenced
by nature, creating glass more beautiful
than Tiffany, Paris celebrated your work
at the Louvre as you paid homage to
Judaism after a journey to Israel even
though it was not your religion nor homeland.

OH, MUNCH, WHAT WERE YOU THINKING

when you saw
*a huge endless
scream course
through nature?*

existing in four
versions too many
macabre self-
portraits echo fear.

both our fathers
mentally ill, seeds
of insanity run
through our roots.

reverberating waves
resonate in brush-
strokes of a figure
on a bridge, hands

like question marks
cradle horrified
expression not
abstract, but real.

GARDEN OF MY HOSPITAL

makes me sigh. I
imagined it would

be this. You
never served time

in a Kentucky
mental institution.

IN ANCIENT GREECE, SOPHISTS

measure the existence of truth
as individual not universal; not absolute
Aristotle's father and my grandfather
both physicians, yet Plato's student blessed
with orphanage, blasphemous words
unless spoken by an insignificant girl.
I do not have the Oedipus privilege of gouging
my eyes I need to read Aristotle's writings
on nature making him the world's first scientist

when I am the last to understand and only learned
through Whitman's *leaves of grass* transcendental
truth. I revere martyrs like Socrates executed
for corrupting youth and Holden Caulfield whose
merry-go-round Odyssean journey searching
an oracle in Phoebe futile; although the sentiment

appreciated as I practice Plato's philosophy
of aesthetics, a branch he invented I teach
as an excuse to day dream in paintings
drenched in exuberance Van Gogh graces
the pages of the art history text I leaf ahead
(abandon Doric, Ionic, Corinthian) to look
at starry nights and potato eaters, again.

SUNDAY AFTERNOON AT THE MUSEUM

When first, I see your painting outside
      a book, hanging on a wall,
      I reach to brush the mystery
      of layers I know are underneath
      until a blue uniformed arm
      intercepts my ten-year-old
      touch before alarm sounds.

I turn to follow an enchanted
      path my own desire carved
      into crowds to see, *really see,*
      every painting with my own
      artist eyes searching for answers.

SATURDAY EVENING

> A writer should write with his eyes and a painter paint with his ears.
>
> —Gertrude Stein

Candle lights butter-
colored plaster-
cracked walls as
backdrop in Salon

for interesting work
from Spaniard's new
painter friend everyone

clamors to see.

Such a bother.

Only one evening all
we afford until Henri says,

When I put a green, it is not grass.
When I put a blue, it is not the sky.

I am delighted enough
to open my home.

I STUMBLE UPON LES DEMOISELLES D'AVIGNON

and gasp   at its sheer size
       hanging
               in MoMa
   one
       September
           afternoon
(when New York is crisp)

and I momentarily   forget what
                you
                             thought to offer.

As I cry   cubist tears   in response
      remembering   why I adore thee,

                     (Spaniard painter)   from the first
time I   wandered Barcelona
    searching   for your early

      line drawings so complete

parsimony   not even a word
     to describe   their beauty evolved

into what   just might be   most

      beautiful   (or grotesque)

of form   based upon   African masks
Matisse first   gave you as gifts

        to abandon   exquisite tradition

        to explore   facets unnatural.
I cannot
    turn   away for an hour
      gazing   at *a field of broken glass.*

FOR ALL THE WORLD

    All I know is something like a bird within her sang.
                                              —Robert Hunter

you paid
owners
to set
their caged
birds free
in hopes
to soar
yourself
sketching
fluttering
wings,
ambitious
inventions
to move
mountains
and swim
deeply below.
Wandering
projects
in notebooks
thousands
of pages
of sketches
when no
more than
twenty
paintings
still
survive,
although
your *Mona*

hung
in Napoleon's
boudoir centuries
before I barely
caught
glimpse
behind glass,
caged
at the Louvre.
How small
a portrait
of nobody
special
would
attract all
the world's
attention.

TWITTERING MACHINE
for Julie

ideographic fascination
fairy tale dreamer paints

beyond the scope to imitate
sentimental bird song mocking

our faith in miracles of machine
sinister lures of striking invention

only a few lines of ink dabbed
with watercolor simplicity engage

our attention from its title to
your composition complete

MAD MAN

> male mother of methodical madness
>
> —Max Ernst

Confusing birds and humans
for years after death of your pet
cockatoo,   experiencing dreams
hallucinogenic   stemming from
measles may   account for your
passion to look   inward, inducing
visions you   turned into paintings
surreal. You invented frottage,
new method   for generating
surprising imagery influences
Dali to melt clocks and
Margritte to impose
blue skies within
one eye.

EMPEROR

I've seen so many
insects, but not   as often

to not only sketch,
but to paint   a moth

how common
a bug to draw

your concentration

WHAT EXACTLY IS SEURAT'S POINT?

Tiny little dots of paint not necessarily the point
of perspective to capture an afternoon of leisure

irony of labor to composition creating a world
I have little interest in entering. Its beauty less

fleeting than the gusts of wind that propel
sailboats across placid blue water and I wonder

why these women in corsets and bustles
holding umbrellas and wearing hats to protect

their privilege of position because to be dark
would be contemptuous and I rail against

unintentional racism found over one hundred
years later as I gaze with contempt and little

apology for your work, Sir.

FLUX OF LIVING

Renoir, where did you find eternal optimism
saying, *life a perpetual holiday* I have found

to be true in *Le Moulin de la Galette?* Was it
your refusal to use the color black in your work

that staved off despair when you were so broke,
you squeezed tubes of paint hoping for one last

drop? You claim black punches holes into canvas
choosing to use blues for shadows, dappling white

sunspots and having the nerve to snip figures
of edge to invite viewers into an implied

scene I so want to enter, enchanted by your six
month commitment to capture revelry and my

heart breaks arthritis so crippled you, paintbrush
strapped to your hand to continue to work

confined in a wheelchair. Even Matisse laid
down his brushes for scissors.

ABSTRACT LOSS

Rothko, perhaps you should
have studied Renoir when

you fell so far into depression,
you took your own life. How

sad the world was deprived
more of your color fields. Did

eradicating all evidence of
brush strokes lead you to drink

or did your melancholy stem

from a deeper place of Russian
heritage?

BASQUIAT! RADIANT CHILD

Haitian-Puerto Rican son
spiritual descendant of the Dutch painter
sharing the same fate
birth after death of your brothers

Vincent signed his canvas
to mimic his brother's gravestone
you, Jean-Michel, signed SAMO

Lower Manhattan your canvas
before encoded text, cartography of your own kind
standing in paint-splattered Armani, brush in hand
resurrecting Nubian slaves as reminders of history
    (to white liberal feminists)
scraping *Gray's Anatomy* collage images
gift from your mother insane inheritance
before heroin resurrected your soul

from legacy of colonial enterprise interwoven
text within your locks transformed into paintings
within the space of only eight years
member of 27 Club not solace enough

chasing the dragon in sunny Los Angeles
to the Ivory Coast ending finally
on your ranch in Hawaii
Afro-Atlantic traditional art
not enough to sustain
beyond your friendship
with Andy tragically lost
to the decade
you sought to escape

FOURTH DIMENSION

> More than ever I detest the things in which I have success at the first attempt.
>
> —Claude Monet

last task of haystacks too easy
thirty canvases the first
series in the history of painting

the protagonist time

unpredictable movement

your labor lauded pinnacle
of Impressionism captures

shadows of twenty-four hours

four seasons and two years

in the second-floor apartment
gazing through the window
you stood days, paintbrush

ten canvases simultaneously examining

changing light, shadow, image

movement, atmosphere of time
your original idea demonstrates
tenacious brilliance because

you finished

GOOD NIGHT

> I don't know anything with certainty, but seeing the stars makes me dream.
>
> —Vincent van Gogh

we cannot write what we know
so well—any poem will be too
cliché, Vincent. Songs scribbled
starry night—books devoted to
the last painting before you (almost)
failed—yet succeeded suicide—
how charmed I still am by this work,
yet this poem does not deserve
a page

COULD THIS BE TRUE?

New information
for my forty-eight-
year-old brain that
you didn't shoot
yourself. Took
blame for a teen
and his sibling
pulling the trigger
you shed yourself
of financial burden
to Theo, not
knowing he would
follow you to death
a mere six months
later. No matter. How
could I have never
known? Assumed
suicide in stride.
Martyr to painting
torturous hours
in unforgiving fields.
Did the teen ever
forgive himself?

Theo followed
too soon
wife and child
left behind merely
six months after
losing Vincent.
What inspired
her to promote
paintings? I

wonder if
I would ever
be that true.

INSTRUCT

sudents to lie
under desk
only one hour,
not four years
like Michelangelo
painting ceiling
plaster falling
dust clogging
squeezing life.

They must color
image taped
to belly of desk
on their backs
to feel muscles
strain and fingers
cramp before
we tromp outside,
sit on blankets
and ponder sky
like Turner who
adored the clouds.

I ask them
to search
for an ordinary
rock to paint
secret desire
in primitive
symbols to place
around classroom
until wish fulfilled
to remember power

of cave paintings
alchemy of first art.

Celebrate arrival
of spring in abstract
expressionism because
who doesn't love
to fling paint
splattering canvas
with abandon?

After dismissal,
silence descends
causing me to climb
stairs to own studio
facing blank canvas
on easel anticipating
familiar motion
of my brush caressing
its surface, coaxing
color, form, texture—
the universe I still
inhabit.

RESOURCES

Ancient History Encyclopedia Limited. 2009–2019. "Christine de Pizan." https://www.ancient.eu/Christine_de_Pizan/.

The Art Story Foundation. 2019. "Paul Cézanne." *The Art Story: Modern Art Insight*. https://www.theartstory.org/artist-cezanne-paul.htm.

Boucher, Brian. 3 October 2017. "Has Duchamp's Final Work Harbored a Secret for Five Decades? This Artist Says Yes." *Art Net News*. https://news.artnet.com/art-world/duchamp-etant-donnes-secret-serkan-ozkaya-1103216.

Bradshaw Foundation. 2019. "Lascaux: Cave Paintings of Southwestern France." http://www.bradshawfoundation.com/lascaux/.

The Broad. 2018. "Jean-Michel Basquiat." https://www.thebroad.org/art/jean%E2%80%90michel-basquiat.

Brooklyn Museum. 2004–2019. "Artemisia Gentileschi." https://www.brooklynmuseum.org/eascfa/dinner_party/place_settings/artemisia_gentileschi.

———. ———. "The Dinner Party by Judy Chicago." https://www.brooklynmuseum.org/exhibitions/dinner_party.

Caravaggio.org. 2009–2019. *Caravaggio and His Paintings*. https://www.caravaggio.org/.

Carone, Angela. 7 February 2014. "Christo Talks About His Artwork, Jeanne-Claude And Garlic." https://www.kpbs.org/news/2014/feb/05/christo-talks-about-his-artwork-jeanne-claude-and-/.

Chicago/Woodman, LLC. 2019. *Judy Chicago*. http://www.judychicago.com/.

Chihuly, Inc. 2019. https://www.chihuly.com/.

Christo. 2019. *Christo and Jeanne-Claude*. https://christojeanneclaude.net/.

ClaudeMonetGallery.org. 2002–2017. *Claude Oscar Monet: The Complete Works*. https://www.claudemonetgallery.org/.

The Dorothea Tanning Foundation. 2013. *Dorothea Tanning*. https://www.dorotheatanning.org/index.

Edgar-Degas.org. 2002–2017. *Edgar Degas: The Complete Works*. https://www.edgar-degas.org/.

Encyclopedia Britannica. 2019. "Christine de Pisan." https://www.britannica.com/biography/Christine-de-Pisan.

Finnan, Vincent. 2008–2019. "Hieronymus Bosch: The first Surrealist?" https://www.italian-renaissance-art.com/Hieronymus-Bosch.html.

Franciscan Media. 2019. "Saint Hildegard of Bingen." https://www.franciscanmedia.org/saint-hildegard-of-bingen/.

Frida-Kahlo-Foundation.org. 2002–2017. *Frida Kahlo: The Complete Works*. https://www.frida-kahlo-foundation.org/.

Fundació Joan Miró. 2019. *The Fundació Joan Miró*. https://www.fmirobcn.org/en/foundation/.

Georgia O'Keeffe Museum. 2019. https://www.okeeffemuseum.org/.

Hieronymus-Bosch.org. 2002–2017. *Hieronymus Bosch: The Complete Works*. https://www.hieronymus-bosch.org/.

Hopkin, Owen. 2019. "Hildegard of Bingen: life and music of the great female composer." https://www.classicfm.com/composers/bingen/guides/discovering-great-composers-hildegard-von-bingen/.

Husker, Jan and Phyllis Freeman. 1980. *The Complete Van Gogh: Paintings, Drawings, Sketches*. New York: Harrison House.

Independent. n.d. "Vincent van Gogh." https://www.independent.co.uk/topic/VincentVanGogh.

Jackson-Pollock.org. 2002–2017. *Jackson Pollock and His Paintings*. https://www.jackson-pollock.org/

Jan-Van-Eyck.org. 2002–2017. *Jan van Eyck or Johannes de Eyck: The Complete Works*. http://www.jan-van-eyck.org/.

Janson, H. W., and Patricia Egan. 1986. *History of Art. 3rd Edition*. New York: Harry N. Abrams, Inc.

Janson, Leo, Hans Luijten, and Nienke Bakker. n.d. "Vincent van Gogh: The Letters." http://vangoghletters.org/vg/.

Jones, Jonathan. 30 November 2011. "Leonardo da Vinci unleashed: the animal rights activist within the artist." *The Guardian*. https://www.theguardian.com/artanddesign/jonathanjonesblog/2011/nov/30/leonardo-da-vinci-animal-rights-activist.

Kino, Carol. 13 January 2009. "Coosje van Bruggen, Sculptor, Dies at 66." *New York Times*. https://www.nytimes.com/2009/01/13/arts/13vanbruggen.html.

Leman, Kristina. 15 February 1995, created; 24 May 1995, modified. "The Life and Works of Hildegard von Bingen (1098–1179)." *Fordham University Medieval Sourcebook*. https://sourcebooks.fordham.edu/med/hildegarde.asp.

Masterworks Fine Arts Gallery. n.d. "Henri Matisse Biography." https://www.masterworksfineart.com/artists/henri-matisse/biography.

McKay, John P., Bennett D. Hill, and John Buckler. 1983. *A History of Western Society*, 2nd Edition. Boston: Houghton Mifflin.

Metropolitan Museum of Art. 2000–2019. https://www.metmuseum.org/.

———. ———. "Haystacks (Effect of Snow and Sun),1891, Claude Monet." https://www.metmuseum.org/art/collection/search/437122.

Ministère de la Culture. 2018. *Lascaux*. http://archeologie.culture.fr/lascaux/en.

Moonan, Wendy. 8 May 2015. "Why Elaine de Kooning Sacrificed Her Own Amazing Career for Her More-Famous Husband's." *Smithsonian.com*. https://www.smithsonianmag.com/smithsonian-institution/why-elaine-de-kooning-sacrificed-her-own-amazing-career-her-more-famous-husbands-180955182/.

Munchmuseet. n.d. "The Life of Edvard Munch." https://munchmuseet.no/en/munch.

The Museum of Modern Art. 2019. https://www.moma.org/.

———. ———. "Mark Rothko." https://www.moma.org/artists/5047.

———. ———. "Paul Klee, *Twittering Machine (Die Zwitscher-Maschine)*, 1922." https://www.moma.org/collection/works/37347.

The National Gallery. 2019. "Michelangelo Merisi da Caravaggio." https://www.nationalgallery.org.uk/artists/michelangelo-merisi-da-caravaggio.

National Gallery of Art. 2018. "Edgar Degas." https://www.nga.gov/features/slideshows/edgar-degas.html.

———. ———. "Hieronymus Bosch." https://www.nga.gov/collection/artist-info.986.html.

National Museum of Women in the Arts. 2019. "Judy Chicago." https://www.nmwa.org/explore/artist-profiles/judy-chicago.

———. ———. "Rosa Bonheur." https://nmwa.org/explore/artist-profiles/rosa-bonheur.

Oldenburg, Claes, and Coosje van Bruggen. n.d. http://www.oldenburgvanbruggen.com/.

Olsen, Annikka. 24 July 2018. "21 Facts About Marc Chagall." https://www.sothebys.com/en/articles/21-facts-about-marc-chagall.

Park West Gallery. 2008–2018. "Marc Chagall." https://www.parkwestgallery.com/artist/marc-chagall/.

Paul-Klee.org. 2016. "Twittering Machine." http://www.paul-klee.org/twittering-machine/.

Pierre-Auguste-Renoir.org. 2002–2017. *Pierre Auguste Renoir: The Complete Works*. https://www.pierre-auguste-renoir.org/.

Pirani, Fiza. 18 December 2018. "Who was Paul Klee? Google honors iconic German-Swiss artist." *The Atlanta Journal-Constitution*. https://www.ajc.com/news/world/who-was-paul-klee-google-honors-iconic-german-swiss-artist/WTrejBnI1WfLW6gCHlNjoL/.

Poetry Foundation. 2019. "Gertrude Stein." https://www.poetryfoundation.org/poets/gertrude-stein.

Rosasco, Betsy. 2019. "Works by Gabriele Münter." *The Princeton University Art Museum.* https://artmuseum.princeton.edu/story/works-gabriele-m%C3%BCnter.

San Francisco Museum of Modern Art. 2019. "Paul Klee." https://www.sfmoma.org/artist/Paul_Klee/.

Sanouillet, Anne. n.d. "Marcel Duchamp." *Dada & the Dada Movement.* https://www.dadart.com/dadaism/dada/035a-duchamp-cage.html

The Solomon R. Guggenheim Foundation. 2019. "Jean Arp." https://www.guggenheim.org/artwork/artist/jean-arp.

———. ———. "Paul Klee." https://www.guggenheim.org/artwork/artist/Paul-Klee.

Sporre, Dennis J. 2000. *The Creative Impulse: An Introduction to the Arts.* 5th Edition. Englewood Cliffs, New Jersey: Prentice-Hall Inc.

Stoner Productions. 1999. "… The Myth of Mona Lisa." *Treasures of the World.* https://www.pbs.org/treasuresoftheworld/mona_lisa/mlevel_1/m4myth.html.

Strickland, Carol. 1992. *The Annotated Mona Lisa: A Crash Course in Art History from Prehistoric to Post-Modern.* Kansas City: Andrews McMeel.

Tate. 2019. "Frottage." https://www.tate.org.uk/art/art-terms/f/frottage.

———. ———. Marc Chagall." https://www.tate.org.uk/art/artists/marc-chagall-881.

———. ———. "Marcel Duchamp." https://www.tate.org.uk/art/artists/marcel-duchamp-1036.

Tesler, Ugo Filippo, M.D. 2012. "The History of Art versus the Art of Surgery." *Texas Heart Institute Journal,* 39(6): 825–830. https://www.ncbi.nlm.nih.gov/pmc/articles/PMC3528222/.

TheMiddleAges.Net. 2014. "Christine de Pisan." http://www.themiddleages.net/people/christine_pisan.html.

The Van Gogh Gallery. n.d. https://www.vangoghgallery.com/.

Van Gogh Museum. n.d. https://www.vangoghmuseum.nl/en.

WassilyKandinsky.net. 2008–2019. "Gabriele Münter." https://www.wassilykandinsky.net/gabrielemunter.php.

Weinberg, H. Barbara. October 2004. "Mary Stevenson Cassatt (1844–1926)." *Heilbrunn Timeline of Art History.* https://www.metmuseum.org/TOAH/HD/cast/hd_cast.htm.

WETA. March 2005. *The Life and Times of Frida Kahlo: A Film by Amy Stechler.* https://www.pbs.org/weta/fridakahlo/life/.

Will, Barbara. March/April 2012. "The Strange Politics of Gertrude Stein." *Humanities: The Magazine of the National Endowment for the Humanities.* https://www.neh.gov/humanities/2012/marchapril/feature/the-strange-politics-gertrude-stein.

ACKNOWLEDGMENTS

I am deeply grateful to Jay McCoy for his endless patience and careful notes in seeing this manuscript to completion. Thank you, Katerina Stoykova, for wading through years of drafts with your gentle guidance and sharp eye. You are my owl. Special thanks to Daniel Klemer for his care in polishing this book, much like a sculptor buffs marble to sheen. I am forever grateful to Clevelle Scherer, my first art teacher who provided me a sanctuary where I learned to paint and draw. I have such fond memories of your home. I would not have been able to find my voice in the stacks of research without airing my poems to Chris Davis and Julie Silverman. Thank you both for your friendship. Ivy Thompson, our trip to the Louvre and Ferris wheel adventures in Paris bring such joyous memories. Kevin Neumann, you are the love of my life. Without your encouragement and belief in me as an artist, none of this would be possible. Finally, this collection is for Carter, the sun; oh, my son.

The author is grateful to the editors of the literary publications in which the following poems first appeared:

"Victor over Medieval Misogyny," "The Viriditas of Hildegard of Bingen (1098–1179)," "*Venus of Willendorf* Charmed Stone": *Trivia: The Feminist Issue* 2014

"Joyful Exit": *Circe's Lament*, Accents Publishing 2015

"A Woman's Shepard": *& Grace*, Accents Publishing 2015

"Ars Poetica Writer's Block (Go Around)" and "Kandinsky *Composition IV* What is true?": *Ekprastic.Net* 2015

"Basquiat! Radiant Child": *HIV Here & Now* (website), Indolent Books 2016

"Ode to a Roman Sarcophagus": *The Children of Orpheus Anthology* 2016

"Kindred Spirits": *The Messenger is Sudden Thunder Anthology*, Accents Publishing 2016

"In Ancient Greece, Sophists," "Oh, Munch, What Were You Thinking": *Let's Talk About It Anthology*, League of Minnesota Poets 2019

ABOUT THE AUTHOR

Elizabeth Beck is a writer, artist and teacher who lives with her family on a pond in Lexington, Kentucky. *Painted Daydreams: Collection of Ekphrastic Poems* is her third book. Elizabeth achieved her B.A. in English Literature with a minor in Fine Arts from the University of Cincinnati and her M.Ed. from Xavier University. She is an award-winning English and Art History teacher. During her time at Withrow High School, she founded *The Tracks* literary magazine. She is the proud recipient of an Artist Enrichment grant through the Kentucky Foundation for Women. November 2011, Elizabeth founded The Teen Howl Poetry Series that serves the youth of Central Kentucky. In 2015, she founded Leestown OUT LOUD spoken word group in her capacity as Drama Teacher at Leestown Middle School.

www.ingramcontent.com/pod-product-compliance
Lightning Source LLC
Chambersburg PA
CBHW020125130526
44591CB00032B/531